D1557780

Spotlight on
ANCIENT CIVILIZATIONS
EGYPT

# The Ancient Egyptian ECONOMY

Leigh Rockwood

Published in 2014 by The Rosen Publishing Group, Inc.
29 East 21st Street, New York, NY 10010

First Edition

Editor: Jennifer Way
Book Design: Kate Vlachos
Layout Design: Colleen Bialecki

Photo Credits: Cover, p. 22 DEA/G. Dagli Orti/Contributor/De Agostini/Getty Images; p. 5 Leemage/Universal Images Group/Getty Images; pp. 6, 7, 13, 14, 16, 17 (top), 19, 21 DEA/G. Dagli Orti/De Agostini Picture Library/Getty Images; p. 8 Werner Forman/Contributor/Universal Images Group/Getty Images; pp. 9, 11, 20 Egyptian/The Bridgeman Art Library/Getty Images; p. 10 pavalena/ Shutterstock.com; p. 12 Jane Rix/Shutterstock.com; p. 15 Paul Vinten/Shutterstock. com; p 17 (bottom) © 2001 Francis Dzikowski, p. 18 Elena Elisseeva/Shutterstock. com.

Library of Congress Cataloging-in-Publication Data

Rockwood, Leigh.
 The ancient Egyptian economy / by Leigh Rockwood. — 1st ed.
    p. cm. — (Spotlight on ancient civilizations: Egypt)
Includes index.
 ISBN 978-1-4777-0765-4 (library binding) — ISBN 978-1-4777-0863-7 (pbk.) — ISBN 978-1-4777-0864-4 (6-pack)
1. Egypt—Economic conditions—To 332 B.C.—Juvenile literature. 2. Material culture—Egypt—Juvenile literature. 3. Industries—Egypt—Juvenile literature. I. Title. II. Series: Spotlight on ancient civilizations. Egypt.
DT61.R536 2014
330.932—dc23

                                        2012049623

Manufactured in the United States of America

CPSIA Compliance Information: Batch #S13PK2: For Further Information contact Rosen Publishing, New York, New York at 1-800-237-9932

# CONTENTS

# Agriculture and Industry

**Agriculture** made up a major part of ancient Egypt's economy. Agriculture thrived because Egypt has a **climate** that is warm year-round, and the Nile River's yearly flooding provided Egyptians with as many as three harvests each year.

Ancient Egypt also had many natural resources, including flax, papyrus, stone, and gold. These materials were used to make cloth, paper, buildings, and jewelry. This led to the rise of industries with merchants and craftsmen creating and selling these goods. This book will explore how Egypt's natural resources created a strong and varied economy and made this empire one of the ancient world's richest **civilizations**.

This tomb painting shows officials recording information about a wheat harvest. Ancient Egyptians kept good records of the crops and goods they produced.

# The Agricultural Economy

Agriculture helped bring wealth to ancient Egypt.
Farmers grew grains such as barley, corn, and wheat.
They also grew a wide variety of fruits and vegetables
such as onions, beans, dates, figs, cucumbers, grapes,
and melons. Cattle and sheep provided meat and milk.
In addition, animals like oxen were used in farmwork
and helped increase the amount of land that could be
worked and the amount of crops grown.

The farmworker in this tomb
painting is harvesting grain.
Barley was ancient Egypt's
biggest grain crop.

Ancient Egyptians kept many of the same farm animals people keep today. The man on the right is milking a cow.

**Surplus** crops provided Egypt with materials to **export** or trade with other countries. This added wealth to the economy and helped boost the growth of other industries and businesses in ancient Egypt.

# Bartering

Much of the trade in ancient Egypt happened through **bartering**. This is when people trade goods and services instead of using money. For example, a farmer earned his pay in the form of sacks of grain. He might barter grain for cloth or other goods.

Here, metalworkers are weighing gold. The value of gold in deben was used to set prices for bartering. One deben worth of gold weighed about 3 ounces (85 g).

Fishermen, like the one shown in this wall carving, bartered their catch. They might trade some of their catch for grain or other goods.

Coins were not used in ancient Egypt until about 500 BC. Before that time, there existed a system in which metals such as gold were given values based on their weight. This unit of weight was called a deben. Deben was not used to buy things. Instead, it was used to set the value of goods and services for bartering.

# Foreign Trade

Ancient Egypt traded with foreign lands, too. It traded with the lands surrounding the Mediterranean and Red seas, as well as other neighboring lands. Important exports included crops and the goods produced by craftspeople in Egypt's industries. These goods included pottery, linen cloth made from the flax plant, and paper made from papyrus.

On this map of today's Egypt, you can see the Mediterranean and Red seas as well as the Nile River. These waterways provided ancient Egypt with trade routes.

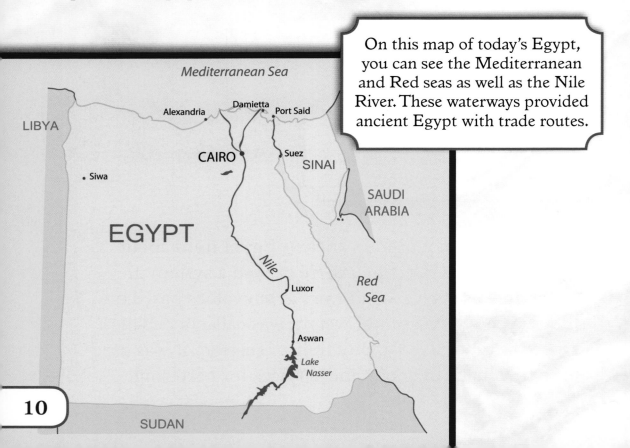

Pottery made in ancient Egypt was a
popular product in other countries.

Gold was an especially valuable export for Egypt. That
is because while gold was found in many parts of Egypt,
the metal was rare elsewhere. Egyptians traded for and
valued goods that were rare in their country. These goods
included iron, silver, wood, and spices.

# Papyrus and Paper

The papyrus plant grew along the Nile. It was an important product in ancient Egypt's economy. Papyrus could be used to make boats and baskets. Paper was the most important product made from papyrus, though. It was invented around 3000 BC and was one of Egypt's main exports.

**Papyrus Plants**

Ancient Egyptians wove the papyrus plant into baskets like the ones these men are using to carry grain.

Egypt was the only civilization that knew how to make paper. Ancient Egyptians wanted to keep other nations from learning to make paper so that demand for it would stay high. The next civilization to create paper was China, which began making paper from bamboo around AD 100.

# Bricks and Pottery

Even mud was an important part of ancient Egypt's economy! Mud from the Nile River's banks was used to make bricks for buildings. Brickmakers did not need much training to learn this trade. Because of this, ancient Egyptians considered this a lowly job, even though bricks were needed for all kinds of buildings.

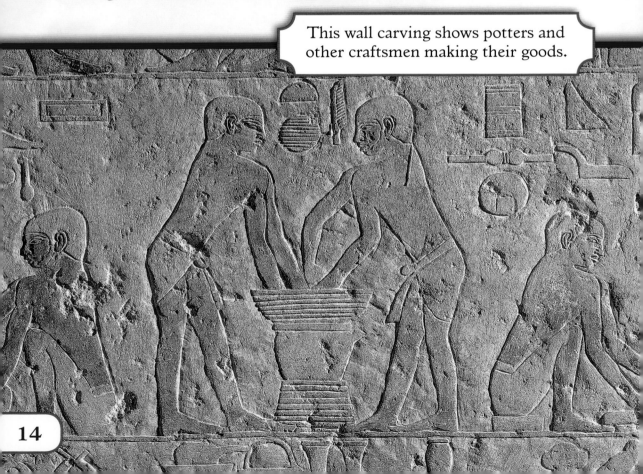

This wall carving shows potters and other craftsmen making their goods.

The Nile River's banks provided ancient Egyptians with the raw materials for pottery and brickmaking.

Clay from the Nile's banks was used by craftsmen to make pottery such as vases, bowls, and cups. These craftsmen were considered manual laborers because pottery was an everyday product. Ancient Egyptians from all walks of life used this pottery. It was also exported to other lands.

# Stonework

Ancient Egypt had plentiful limestone and granite. Stonecutters carved statues and built **temples, tombs,** and pyramids that honored the **pharaohs** and the upper classes. Stonecutting was a highly skilled and valued industry in ancient Egypt.

This is a stone jar. Stonework was special and used in tombs. Pottery made of clay was for everyday use.

*Left*: It took a highly skilled craftsman to carve a detailed stone statue like the one shown here.
*Below*: This is a view from above of the tombs and temples built for the pharaoh Ramses II. This huge set of buildings would have had lots of stoneware and statues among its riches.

Although people from the lower classes did not have statues or stone tombs, they bought stoneware. Stoneware is vases, pots, and jugs made from stone. These things were valuable and were often saved to be buried with people. They were meant for a person's afterlife instead of being used in daily life.

# Cloth Making

The flax plant was plentiful in ancient Egypt. It was the raw material for making a cloth called linen. Linen is soft and light, which made it an ideal fabric for Egypt's hot, dry climate.

## Flax Plants

This linen tunic, or long shirt, belonged to an Egyptian government official named Nakhti.

Many people grew their own flax and wove linen at home. Ancient Egypt also had a linen industry. This was an industry in which women could work. They would work in shops, where they spun thread and wove it into cloth. The finished product could then be sold either within the country or for export.

# Jewelry

People from all classes wore jewelry such as rings and **amulets**. Ancient Egyptians believed that jewelry had protective qualities. Jewelry was in demand, and the craftsmen who made it were valued for their skill.

These bracelets are made of gold and a stone called lapis lazuli.

Gold and some gems, such as turquoise, were plentiful in Egypt. Other metals and gems, such as silver and diamonds, were rare. If they were to be used, they had to be **imported** and were more costly. Craftsmen also made jewelry out of **faience** beads, which had a gemlike appearance. Faience jewelry became a popular foreign export product.

This carving is an amulet made of faience. It is of the god called Khnum, the god of the Nile River.

# Metal and Civilization

Metals are important to civilization. Ancient Egypt's metal industry developed more slowly than its other industries. While ancient Egypt had plentiful gold and copper, it lacked iron. Iron is a strong metal that is good for making tools and weapons.

Ancient Egypt's other important resources, such as flax, gold, and papyrus, helped it develop its economy. This helped Egypt grow into one of the most powerful civilizations in the ancient world.

These ancient Egyptian knives, axes, and other tools are made from bronze. Bronze is a strong metal made from melting together copper and tin.

# GLOSSARY

**agriculture** (A-grih-kul-cher) The science of producing crops and raising livestock, or animals.

**amulets** (AM-yeh-lets) Things worn as good-luck charms.

**bartering** (BAR-tur-ing) Trading.

**civilizations** (sih-vih-lih-ZAY-shunz) People living in a certain way.

**climate** (KLY-mut) The kind of weather a certain place has.

**export** (ek-SPORT) To send something to another place to be sold.

**faience** (fay-AHNTS) Glazed, colored earthenware.

**imported** (im-PORT-ed) Brought in from another country for sale or use.

**pharaohs** (FER-ohz) Ancient Egyptian rulers.

**surplus** (SUR-plus) More than enough.

**temples** (TEM-pelz) Places where people go to worship.

**tombs** (TOOMZ) Graves.

# INDEX

# WEBSITES

Due to the changing nature of Internet links, PowerKids Press has developed an online list of websites related to the subject of this book. This site is updated regularly. Please use this link to access the list: www.powerkidslinks.com/sace/econ/